THE BIG FEELINGS
Book *for* Children

THE BIG FEELINGS
Book *for* Children

Mindfulness Moments to Manage Anger, Excitement, Anxiety, and Sadness

written by SHARON SELBY, MA
illustrated by ANNA HURLEY

ROCKRIDGE
PRESS

For general information on our other products and services or to obtain technical support, please contact our Customer Care Department within the United States at (866) 744-2665, or outside the United States at (510) 253-0500.

Rockridge Press publishes its books in a variety of electronic and print formats. Some content that appears in print may not be available in electronic books, and vice versa.

Interior and Cover Designer: Regina Stadnik
Art Producer: Sara Feinstein
Editor: Barbara J. Isenberg
Production Editor: Rachel Taenzler
Production Manager: Jose Olivera

Illustrations © 2021 Anna Hurley. Author photo courtesy of Carrie Marshall.

Paperback ISBN: 978-1-63878-149-3 | eBook ISBN: 978-1-63878-261-2
R0

Printed in Canada

For all children and their big feelings.
For all adults who care for children
and their big feelings.

CONTENTS

When You're Feeling ANXIOUS . . . 21

When You're Feeling SAD . . . 31

Note to Caregivers and Educators

These activities will work best when your child's emotions are rising or coming down. In the peak of their big feelings, it is best to validate your child's feelings, as they will not be able to hear any rational language when the situation is highly escalated.

YOU'RE GOING TO BE OKAY

We all get BIG feelings sometimes. That's okay. Feelings can be hard. They might even feel out of control.

This book will help you deal with your feelings better. There are lots of fun things to help you when you have big feelings.

Mindfulness helps you handle these big feelings. Mindfulness means slowing down and noticing your feelings and thoughts. It also means noticing what is happening around you. Everyone is different. Some tools will help you more than others. You can find your favorites.

When You're Feeling ANGRY . . .

You might feel like you are going to explode when you are angry. Your heart might beat faster. Breathing might be harder. Your mind might be racing. Think about a time when you felt angry. What happened to your body and mind?

There are four different tools in this section to help you deal with your anger:

TRAFFIC LIGHT: See the signal for what to do next.

VOLCANO BREATHING: Let out your fiery anger safely.

THE TRAIN OF THOUGHTS: Pick what thoughts you want to keep.

MAGIC WORDS: Use your words to get help.

Traffic Light

Pretend you are a car. When you feel angry, you go very fast!

Stop and Breathe

You come to a traffic light. It is **RED.** Red means **STOP!** Stop and take a big breath.

Walk Away

Yellow means **SLOW DOWN!**
Walk away.

Quiet Place

Green means **GO!** Go to a quiet place where you can calm down.

Volcano Breathing

You might feel like a volcano when you are angry. Pretend your anger is like lava inside of you. Breathe in a big, deep breath. Hold it. Then breathe out the lava and fire with a huge breath. Do this five times. Use your fingers to count your huge breaths!

The Train of Thoughts

Your thoughts shape how you feel. Pretend your thoughts are a train. Imagine standing at a train station. There are two different trains. You can choose which train you're going to get on.

Do you want to get on a train with thoughts that make you feel angry?

Or do you want to get on a train with thoughts that help you feel calm?

Magic Words

**People will stop and listen when you say,
"I FEEL ANGRY."** Why? Because people care about
your feelings. You'll feel better, too, when you say how
you feel out loud. Give it a try and see what happens!

When You're Feeling EXCITED . . .

It feels good to be excited. But sometimes your excitement can bother others. How do you know if you are *too* excited? You might yell and make lots of noise. You might not wait for your turn to talk. You might get too close to people or grab them without asking. What happens to you when you are really excited?

There are four different tools in this section to help if you feel too excited:

TINGLING HANDS: Rub away your energy.

BUTTERFLY HUG!: Calm down with a nice hug exercise.

3-2-1: SHAKE OUT THE WIGGLES!: Wiggle your way to calm.

JACK-IN-THE-BOX JUMPS!: Let out your excitement.

Tingling Hands

You are made of energy. That energy moves fast when you are excited. You can feel it. Rub your hands together really fast for five seconds. Then, hold your hands a tiny bit apart. Can you feel the energy and excitement flowing away from your fingers? It may also feel like buzzing.

Butterfly Hug!

Cross your arms. Put your hands on your shoulders. Then, tap your left shoulder. Then your right. Keep doing this while you take deep breaths. You can tap slow, medium, or fast. Your eyes can be open or closed. Your tapping hands will look like butterfly wings as you calm down.

3-2-1: Shake Out the Wiggles!

Shake out your energy! Shake your right arm and count to three. Then, shake your left arm and count to three. Next, shake your right leg and count to two. Then shake your left leg and count to two. Give your whole body one big shake to finish. Do the whole thing again if you want!

Jack-in-the-Box Jumps!

It might feel like you are about to burst sometimes. Let your excitement out! Pretend you are a jack-in-the-box toy and crouch down. Count to three. Then, jump as high as you can! Do this five times.

When You're Feeling ANXIOUS . . .

Anxiety is when you feel worried or nervous. Your stomach might hurt. You might shake a little or have a hard time talking. This might happen because your brain gets confused. It thinks you're in danger even if you are not.

There are four tools in this section to help you calm your anxiety:

WASH AWAY THE WORRY WAVE: Picture the ocean.

WEED THE GARDEN: Get rid of worry thoughts.

STARFISH BREATHING: Calm your whole body down.

WHAT'S MY CAN-DO?: Learn what you can control.

Wash Away the Worry Wave

Take a deep breath in. Picture a big pile of worries on the beach. Breathe out and watch a big wave wash your worries away. Breathe in and imagine the big wave rising up again. Then breathe out. Feel the wave wash away your worries. Keep going until you feel better.

Weed the Garden

Your mind is like a garden. The flowers are your
happy thoughts. The weeds are your worry thoughts.

Close your eyes. Imagine pulling the weeds out. This
means pulling out the worry thoughts. What happy
thoughts can you think of?

Starfish Breathing

Being still can help you when you are worried. Lie on your back on the floor. Spread your arms and legs out like a starfish. Take a deep breath in and hold it for three seconds. Let a big breath out. Feel your arms and legs touching the ground. Feel your head and your whole body being supported by the ground. Continue deep breathing until you feel calm.

What's My Can-Do?

Sometimes there are things that are out of your control. But there are often things that you can control. These are things you **CAN** do. Think about your "can-do." For example, starting at a new school might make you nervous. What could be your "can-do"? You could visit your new school before your first day of class.

When You're Feeling SAD . . .

Being sad is a feeling that we all get. It doesn't feel good to feel sad. Let your tears out if you feel like crying. You might feel worse if things stay bottled up inside. You might feel mad before you feel sad. You can also feel mixed feelings, like sad and worried or sad and scared.

There are four different tools in this section to help you with your sad feelings:

EVERY CLOUD HAS A SILVER LINING: Thinking of good things can help.

MY HAPPY PLACE: Think of a safe space that makes you happy.

CIRCLE BREATHING: Deep breaths help you calm down.

STORM CLOUDS: Let your feelings out.

31

Every Cloud Has a Silver Lining

Pretend your sadness is a dark cloud. Now, imagine the sun shining through. It gives the clouds a glittery, silver lining.

The sun is goodness. Thinking of good things can help us feel a little better. What good things are you thankful for?

My Happy Place

Thoughts create feelings. It can be helpful to think of your happy place when you are sad. Where is your happy place? Is it a room in your home? It could be a place in nature or a local park. What do you see, smell, hear, touch, and taste when you think of this place? You can visit this happy place in your mind when you are feeling sad.

Circle Breathing

Our breathing can get quicker when we're sad. It helps to stand up and take a big, deep breath. Make a circle shape with your hands above your head.

Then breathe out and bring your arms down in front of your body.
Make a circle shape again. Do this again as many times as you need to.

Storm Clouds

Tears help your body empty out the storm cloud of sadness. There can be a lot of tears. This is okay. Tears help your body empty out the sadness.

Talking about your sad feelings helps, too. Sad feelings are like stormy weather. They will empty out, pass, and go away.

About the Author

Sharon Selby, MA, is a registered clinical counselor in West Vancouver, British Columbia, Canada, and has been counseling children, teens, and families for the past 24 years. She is also the author of *Surfing the Worry Imp's Wave,* a public speaker, a media consultant, and a writer for a popular blog at SharonSelby.com.

About the Illustrator

Anna Hurley spends most of her time drawing things for fun and profit. She loves bright colors and can often be found playing board games, riding her bike, and eating snacks. She has worked on branding systems, packaging design, and many children's books, and she's also illustrated a plethora of printed paraphernalia. She lives and works in Oakland, California.